Terriers

Laura K. Murray

CREATIVE EDUCATION • CREATIVE PAPERBACKS

seedlings

Published by Creative Education and Creative Paperbacks
P.O. Box 227, Mankato, Minnesota 56002
Creative Education and Creative Paperbacks
are imprints of The Creative Company
www.thecreativecompany.us

Design by Ellen Huber; production by Blue Design
Art direction by Rita Marshall
Printed in the United States of America

Photographs by Corbis (68/George Doyle/Ocean), Dreamstime
(Erik Lam), iStockphoto (Ammit, GlobalP, JoeGough,
Lerche&Johnson, Milan Lipowski, monkeypics, Alex
Potemkin, Alona Rjabceva, s5iźtok, So-CoAddict, sshepard,
taviphoto, Theresasc75, VioletaStoimenova), Shutterstock
(violetblue)

Library of Congress Cataloging-in-Publication Data
Murray, Laura K.
Terriers / Laura K. Murray.
p. cm. — (Seedlings)
Includes bibliographical references and index.
Summary: A kindergarten-level introduction to terriers,
covering their personalities, behaviors, life span, and such
defining features as their paws.
ISBN 978-1-60818-666-2 (hardcover)
ISBN 978-1-62832-251-4 (pbk)
ISBN 978-1-56660-696-7 (eBook)
1. Terriers—Juvenile literature. 2. Dog breeds—Juvenile
literature. [1. Dogs.] I. Title. II. Series: Seedlings.

SF429.T3M87 2016
636.755—dc23   2015007568

CCSS: RI.K.1, 2, 3, 4, 5, 6, 7; RI.1.1,
2, 3, 4, 5, 6, 7; RF.K.1, 3; RF.1.1

First Edition HC 9 8 7 6 5 4 3 2 1
First Edition PBK 9 8 7 6 5 4 3 2 1

TABLE OF CONTENTS

Hello, terriers!

Terriers are breeds of dogs.

They love to dig in the dirt.

7

A terrier is an active pet.

It jumps and barks. It wants to be the boss!

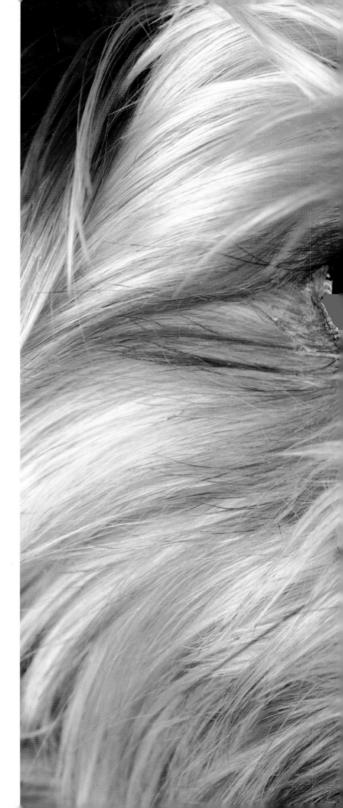

Terrier **coats** can be brown, black, white, and gray.

Yorkshire terriers have long, smooth hair.

Norfolk terriers weigh about 12 pounds. But Airedale terriers (pictured) can weigh 65 pounds!

Terrier puppies eat and play. They use their paws to dig. A pet terrier can live for 10 to 18 years.

Terriers win prizes at dog shows. They chase balls. Then they go to sleep.

Goodbye, terriers!

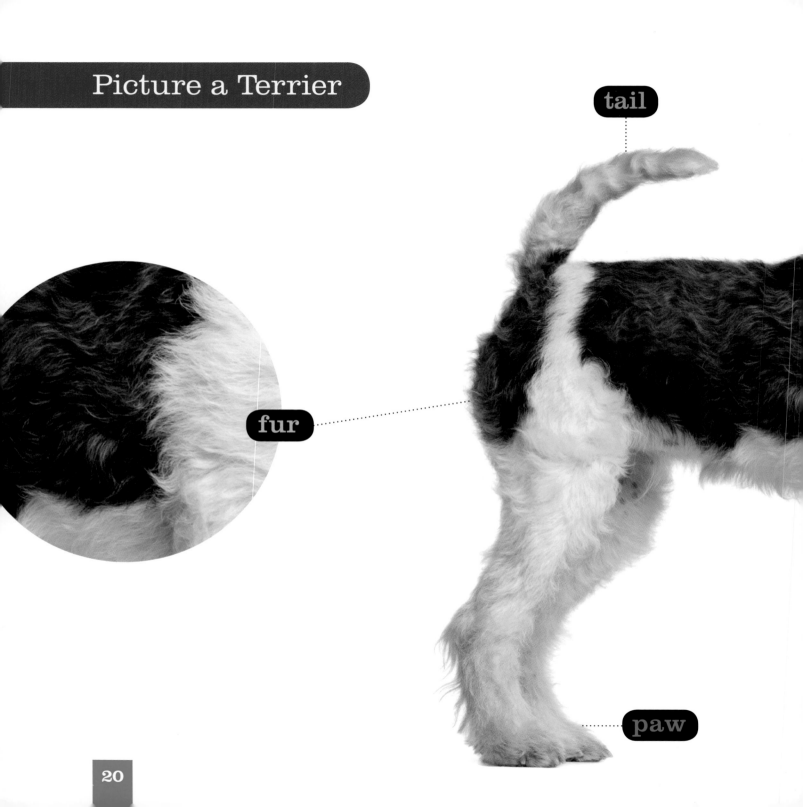

Picture a Terrier

tail

fur

paw

muzzle

mouth

nose

tongue

teeth

leg

21

active: moving a lot and staying busy

breeds: groups of dogs that are alike

coats: fur or hair of an animal

dog shows: contests for dogs

Read More

Green, Sara. *West Highland White Terriers*.
Minneapolis: Bellwether Media, 2010.

Johnson, Jinny. *Yorkshire Terrier*.
Mankato, Minn.: Smart Apple Media, 2013.

Websites

Bailey's Responsible Dog Owner's Coloring Book
https://images.akc.org/pdf/public_education
/coloring_book.pdf
Print out pictures of pet dogs to color.

Terrier Dog Breeds
http://www.animalplanet.com/breed-selector/dog-breeds
/terrier-dogs.html
Look at pictures of different terrier breeds.

Note: Every effort has been made to ensure that the websites listed above are suitable for children, that they have educational value, and that they contain no inappropriate material. However, because of the nature of the Internet, it is impossible to guarantee that these sites will remain active indefinitely or that their contents will not be altered.

23

Index